The ONE Minute Communicator

ONE MINUTE a Week
to
Better Business Communication

Tips, Techniques & Observations

Howard Baker, Jr.

Speakers' Forum
P.O. Box 13997
Salem, OR 97309
(503) 399-8460 & FAX

First Edition
Copyright © 1991 by Howard Baker, Jr.
Cover design by Fredrick Smith
Book title by Michael Nolan
3rd Printing

The ONE MINUTE Communicator

ISBN 0-9623660-1-3
Library of Congress Card Catalog Number 91-071063

Printed in the United States of America

How to Use The ONE MINUTE Communicator

This book was created as a result of hundreds of requests for my practical, common sense coaching tips, techniques and observations for strengthening personal communication without the fear, nervousness and anxiety which most people experience.

The first and most important tip is to utilize **The ONE MINUTE Communicator** over an entire year. Each chapter is designed to be read in less than a minute. You could read the entire book in less than an hour, but you maximize beneficial change by forcing yourself to focus on one chapter a week. Utilize the tip, technique or observation as it best suits your own personal needs—a chapter a week, no more, no less. Don't rush!

Use the chapters as a basis of talk and discussion at weekly staff or office meetings. Use the information, tips, techniques, and observations as a part of your newsletter, bulletin, or bulletin board. Don't infringe on the copyright by failing to credit where you got the information. The key is to use the information over time (one chapter a week).

Learning how to be a better communicator is a lifelong, ongoing task. Strengthening just one aspect of how you communicate affects your entire communication personality. Human communication and interaction continues to be the foundation and "grease" for the wheels and gears of business. The *quality* of our interaction makes the difference. Improved communication isn't a presentation—it's representation!

Watch for the ONE MINUTE clock reminders!

Books by Howard Baker, Jr.

Speech & Speaking Anatomy—unpublished
Cleft Palate—unpublished
Primary Health Care of the Young—Speech and Voice Changes—(contributing author), McGraw-Hill
Communication Power*
Speaker's Choice*
Effective Listening*
Etc ... (Effective Trainers Communicate)*
Effective Personal Communication*
Planning & Preparing Winning Presentations*
Practical Presentation Skills Workshop*
Effective Business Communication*
Putting Your Communication Skills To Work*
Professionally Speaking*
And the CHEAT Goes On. *An Exposé On How Students Are Cheating In School*, Forum Press International
Tricks of the Trade—(contributing author), Houghton-Mifflin
Customer Communication—Technically Speaking*
Technically Speaking—Communication Skills for Technical People*
The ONE MINUTE Listener—in progress

---

* Available from the publisher—Speakers' Forum   Salem, Oregon

Contents

Dedication 7
Acknowledgments 7
From the Author 8

Chapter

1. Ready, Set, Go! 11
2. Angles, Angles, Angles 12
3. Button Up! 13
4. Asides (if you know what I mean) 14
5. Attention! 15
6. Common Communication Problems 16
7. Your Communication Altitude? 17
8. Communication Quotient (C.Q.) 18
9. Head, Chin, Chest & Stomach 19
10. First Impressions 20
11. Style vs. Substance 21
12. Enthusiasm 22
13. Sit vs. Stand 23
14. Pronunciation 24
15. Variety 25
16. Lost Audiences 26
17. Lectern, Podium, Dais, Rostrum 27
18. Meetings 28
19. The Pause Paradox 29
20. Tell, Tell, Tell 30
21. Rhetorical Interrogatives & Non-Words 31
22. Batons & Gesticulations 32
23. The Eyes Have It 33

24. "Counters" Love Redundancies	34
25. Appealing to Others	35
26. Go Toward the Listener	36
27. Writing a Talk	37
28. Movement	38
29. Audience Analysis	39
30. Notes & Manuscripts	40
31. Humor & Laughter	41
32. R.I.P.	42
33. Memorable Openings & Endings	43
34. Monotone	44
35. A PRO Never Goes In Cold!	45
36. Convince Me!	46
37. Question & Answer (Responses)	47
38. Oral Hygiene—Speaker's Breath	48
39. N.I.H. Syndrome	49
40. No COIKs	50
41. Listening Tips—Quick Fix	51
42. "Deadly Dozen" Listening Problems	52
43. Play The Percentages	53
44. Asking vs. Telling	54
45. Match My Predicates	55
46. Visual Aids	56
47. Voice Too Nasal?	57
48. Mumble Mouth	58
49. Overcoming Your Anxiety	59
50. "Mikes"	60
51. Abused Words	61
52. Practice Makes Perfect	62
About the Author	64
ONE MINUTE Communicator Training	65

This Book is Dedicated To:

My loving and supportive mother and father whose continued support, encouragement and humor gives me strength. Thank you for your never-ending stream of book ideas, news clippings and human interest stories. Mom, thanks too for the handmade neckties (I now have over two hundred). I love you.

The lasting joy of my life; my wife Sherrie. Thank you for believing in me and sharing my joy—coaching and helping to make a difference in the world through positive thoughts and deeds ("That's Right!")

The children: Eldon, Heidi, Ashley, Blake, Kimberly and Todd. Your patience with me when I'm being visited by the muse has not always made me as available as I might have been. Thank you for your patience and understanding.

Bill and Virgia Iverson, my in-laws, for your love and inclusion in the family—let's keep on fishin' together, I love it!

Acknowledgment

To those who have helped, aided and guided me on this project. A special thank you to *Steve Cosio* for your ideas and yet another book cover idea. Thank you "Michael the Nolan Man"—*Mike Nolan* for the book title idea and "John the Stern One"—*John Stern* for being there when the title was born and for continued friendship and support. Lastly, a thank you to the tens of thousands of business men and women worldwide who continue to teach me the ways of business communication through my coaching experiences.

From the Author

Over the years my clients have requested I put my common sense, practical, no-nonsense approach to becoming a more effective communicator into a simple book or booklet. This book takes into account the natural and developmental methods by which we all learned to use our most important business tools—our ability to communicate using speech and language. The key concept is for people to use this book to gradually change their perception about business communication. Change your perceptions and you'll change the way you communicate.

The most pressing problem people have about their communication skills is learning how to conquer, deal with, or overcome their nervousness and anxiety. This book holds the keys for mastery of this common problem.

Just as we didn't learn to speak overnight or walk without practice, it is *not* possible to instantly change our communication personality. It requires time as well as practice. **The key to change and improvement is in observing how others communicate.** This book is your guide to informed observation.

Every chapter in this book can be read in less than **ONE MINUTE.** You must then apply what you have read and see if it works for you. Observe those around you professionally as well as personally. There is no such thing as a "gift of gab." Good, effective communicators learn their skills through keen observation over time through trial and error.

The ONE MINUTE Communicator is about helping people reach and realize their potentials. We all have a few "rough edges" which require periodic maintenance (present company included).

Everybody is busy. Don't take time, *make time* to invest in yourself. **ONE MINUTE** at a time, a chapter a week will result in a lifetime of benefits.

Howard Baker, Jr., Salem, Oregon
Business Communication Coach

If we continue doing what we've always done, we deserve to get what we've always got.

Chapter 1   **Ready, Set, Go!**
Ready

Ready means get ready. As you walk to wherever you are going to stand, be sure your entire program is ready. Ready takes moments not minutes.

Erase the board	Adjust lectern
Adjust lighting	Tidy up
Clean easel page	Set-up first overhead

Set

Set means feet. Check foot position then lock it. Stand "stock still" until you have completed the opening portion of your talk. Feet apart less than the width of your shoulders, with one toe one to two inches ahead of the other; feet parallel (if you can).

Go!

First eyes then voice. Let your eyes look out over the group and establish direct eye contact with a few people before you begin speaking.

This is the most powerful magic I know. The magic in **Ready, Set, Go!** is that it lets your audience know immediately that they can relax. You demonstrate to the audience that you have everything under control. Once your audience settles down and quits empathizing, you too will settle down. Learn how to take charge from the outset.

> **Once you've established rapport with the audience, they're yours to enjoy.**

Remember—Make 'em Wait!—Take your time! Don't Rush! Go Slow.

The ONE MINUTE Communicator

Chapter 2 Angles, Angles, Angles

Set means feet! There are two important body angles polished speakers create to soften their image—shoulder angles and a forward leaning body-trunk posture. Both are indirectly related to where you put your feet.

Too close together, no angle.

Too wide, no angle.

Weight Forward—more on the ball of the foot. Knees slightly flexed and not locked.

Feet less than shoulder width apart. Note the slight angle.

Better to error with feet closer together than wider. Foot position is critical—dictates pelvic and shoulder girdle angle and creates a caring, comfortable professional image.

Observation

If you have a picture I.D. or driver's license get it out and look at it. Could there be any relationship as to the quality of your driver's license picture and where your feet were when the picture was taken? Think about it! Squared foot posture translates to a squared shoulder girdle and head posture—stiff and harsh.

| Chapter 3 | Button Up! |

(A gender specific issue of protocol.)

Men First: It is proper to button your top coat button prior to beginning to speak. Not necessary if you are wearing a vested suit—with a vest the option is yours as to whether or not you button your coat prior to beginning to speak.

Women: The same rule does not apply for women wearing business suits. This is partly due to women's fashions which frequently have suit coat buttons but no button holes or may have no buttons or button holes.

> Button your coat prior to starting (part of getting *Ready*). Unbutton once you feel you have gained rapport with the audience. (A personal judgement call—usually after you have concluded your opening remarks.)

Why?
Buttoning the coat helps to make the speaker appear more finished and complete. It also communicates to the audience a change in feeling and mood as the coat is unbuttoned.

Do I have to button my coat? Observe others and make your own decision. Would buttoning the coat have helped create the desired effect? It's a personal judgement call.

There may be times when the coat remains buttoned throughout the entire talk. (For example, formal lectern presentations.)

Begin Like a Pro!
Look Sharp and Crisp.

The ONE MINUTE Communicator

Chapter 4 — Asides
(If you know what I mean!)

Most asides made by speakers involve some degree of negativity about themselves. Asides are words spoken, often times under the breath, to those closest to the speaker and are not heard by the entire group.

Common aside comments:
- "Boy I'm not ready to do this talk today."

- "Sure hope I'm able to pull this off."

- "My writing is so terrible, hope everyone can read what I've written."

- "Gee, that was a terrible talk. I could have done better if I'd practiced."

- Saying "okay" to yourself under your breath.

Regarding Asides:

Keep quiet and don't engage the audience until ready to speak. ***Ready*** *and* ***Set****—done in silence.*

Conversely don't make asides as you leave the front of the room after finishing your talk, especially after you've taken your seat.

Omit the negatives, asides or otherwise. If it's worth saying, say it to the entire audience.

**"Soar Like An Eagle,
Be Positive"**

Howard Baker, Jr. 1969

Chapter 5   "Attention!"

The first order of business is to *grab* the attention of the listener(s). "Move" them out of their current level of attention.

The easiest *attention step* is to use your voice. Increase the intensity (volume), raise the pitch and increase the rate. Let your voice give the first clue as to what your message is about. Be enthusiastic when appropriate.

Attention Steps :
    Rhetorical questions
    Compliment the audience
    Startling fact or statement
    Humorous anecdote
    Narration-Illustration
    Quotation
    Manipulatives
        Prop
        Noise
        Lighting / Altered
    Audience involvement
    Reference to occasion, subject or surroundings

Dare to be Different With Your Attention Step!

Try:

Loud noise	Pantomime
Bring in a prop	Music
Visual	Taped message
Video tape (brief)	
Have a volunteer help you (plan ahead of time)	

"Have the humility to prepare and the self-confidence to bring it off."   Laurence Olivier

Chapter 6   Common Communication Problems

Below is a list of the most common communication problems. How many apply to you?

- [ ] 1.   Nervousness and anxiety—makes audience nervous
- [ ] 2.   Stiff appearance—tight body and voice
- [ ] 3.   No always sure of how to get started
- [ ] 4.   Tells and seldom asks—creates resistance
- [ ] 5.   Too much personal narrative— "I, me, my"
- [ ] 6.   Minimal vocal variety—rate, intensity, pitch
- [ ] 7.   Minimal eye contact and variety of facial expression
- [ ] 8.   Few pauses / phrases—excessive rate
- [ ] 9.   Little or no humor
- [ ] 10.   Boring—too technical, detailed
- [ ] 11.   Excessive movement
- [ ] 12.   Asides, usually negative
- [ ] 13.   Have redundant mannerisms and speech

If you can relate to some of these communication problems, let this book be your weekly guide for one year. Your understanding will change and your communication skills will improve markedly.

Our ability to communicate using speech and language is our most vital tool. It is the number one key to success in business and your personal life. *Speech and language* (verbal and non-verbal) *are our most important business tools.*

Chapter 7 Your Communication *Altitude*?

Adapted from: You Are the Message by Roger Ailes

Are YOU High on Communication? (a self-test)

Score each item from one to five. (1 = low, 5 = high)
Ask someone else to rate you. Compare your score and their score.

Are you / do you?

A. Accept criticism with grace—using the information to change and improve? ☐

B. Confront others without being negative? ☐

C. A self-starter (daily)? ☐

D. Generally, level of enthusiasm? ☐

E. A supportive team player— do you pitch in? ☐

F. Communicate well with fellow employees—both receptive and expressive? ☐

G. Frequently beg off, make excuses and / or pass-the-buck? ☐

H. A solution or a problem at work? (Part of the rumor mill, and gossip spreader?) *(score high if a solution and low if a problem)* ☐

Scores: **Total** ☐

Above 25 — an example for others (highly communicative)
17-24 — time for a straightforward talk with yourself
Below 17 — definitely low altitude

The ONE MINUTE Communicator

Chapter 8   Communication Quotient
(A Self-test)

Answer the following questions.
Have a friend answer the following questions, compare.

	Yes	No
1. Is your physical appearance sharp and crisp?	☐	☐
2. Do you have a sense of humor and laugh easily and often?	☐	☐
3. Are you generally optimistic and enthusiastic?	☐	☐
4. Do you control your rate of speech?	☐	☐
5. Is there variety of rate, intensity and pitch in your speech?	☐	☐
6. Do you have a strong vocabulary?	☐	☐
7. Do you always stand to introduce yourself in a group?	☐	☐
8. Are you able to speak with an audience as opposed to speak to an audience?	☐	☐
9. Do you wait for others to finish talking?	☐	☐
10. Do you use pauses effectively?	☐	☐
11. Have others commented to you about how well you communicate?	☐	☐
12. Do you appear calm before speaking to a group?	☐	☐

10 to 12 "yes" answers —communicator
8 to 9 "yes" answers —potential—practice, practice
5 to 7 "yes" answers —seek opportunities to practice

Chapter 9

Head Up, Also Chin
Chest Out, Stomach In
(Old Quaker Adage)

Trivia Question: Name the bone in the human body that does not connect to any other bone. *(The rest of our bones connect to one another—ankle bone connected to the shin bone, shin bone connected to the thigh bone, etc.)*

We are a society of "benders and stoopers." It is critical that we stand up straight and lift our head slightly. We use the old Quaker adage to remind us how to better posture ourselves.

Head up, also chin does not mean to throw your head back and convey an image of "I'm better than you." Notice that when people are attempting to *look down their nose at you*, they also flair their nostrils. Rather, lift your chin slightly thus allowing your eyes to look more up and out vs. out and down.

Chest out, stomach in does not imply the image of a teenager with a new bra or a military-type posture with the shoulders rigidly pulled back. Instead, lift your sternum (breastbone) slightly. Notice how your abdomen flattens as you elevate your sternum.

A tight shoulder girdle transfers tension to the voice muscles. This subtle hunching of the shoulders is perceived by the listener and conveys nervousness and tension.

> **Demeanor and Style
> Pave the Way For Substance!**

Answer to trivia question.
The hyoid bone is at the root of the tongue and just above the "Adam's Apple" (thyroid cartilage). It has thirty pairs of muscles attached to it. Some of those muscles attach to the shoulder girdle. A relaxed shoulder girdle minimizes the quivering voice and pitch breaks.—Significant!

Chapter 10 — First Impressions

First impressions can be changed but require far more effort. Some say that the first seven seconds are the most critical. I'm not prepared to put such a rigid time limit on first impressions, but there is little doubt as to their importance.

> **You Never Get A Second Chance For A First Impression**

First impressions are more than just appearances and involve dress, style and demeanor. The way others first hear and see us is critical. Who we are and how we come across to others sets the tone for future communicative interaction. Poor first impressions are often difficult or impossible to overcome.

We all read body language. The problem with body language is we want to equate certain body mannerisms with a one-to-one cause or meaning. Body language comes in clusters and it is critical that we read the composite picture.

Learn to talk less, listen more and watch. Let your feelings be your guide as you determine whether or not people's physical actions match their words.

Learn to stand comfortably with your head up. Eye contact is a critical part of a first impression. Street-wise individuals know the value of control through strong eye contact and easily recognize when a person is weak and is uncomfortable.

• You Can't Judge The Book By Its Cover •

Chapter 11 — Style vs. Substance

Most people focus on substance over style. We've been taught how to write and think in order to make sense. For example, the technical presentation seldom lacks technical depth because most people spend plenty of time on the content of what they are going to talk about.

By failing to help our audience feel comfortable we force them to spend time empathizing. While they are empathizing they are less available to absorb our message.

It's critical that we conduct ourself in a way that makes our listener(s) comfortable and available to listen.

**People want to learn and listen
from people whom they perceive
as being friendly, warm and sincere!**

As people sit silently, watching and listening:

> **"Before I care how much you know,
> I want to know how much you care."**

Learn how to get started in a manner which immediately puts listeners at ease. Learn the simple technique of **Ready, Set, Go!** The major benefit comes from practicing **Ready, Set, Go!** You'll find your nervousness and anxiety decrease the more you practice. Let your style convey:

Calm, Cool, Collected, Confident, Control

Be sure your style sets a positive mood for what you are about to say—Style first and then substance.

Chapter 12 — Enthusiasm

There is a famous story about Mark Twain who was not only a renowned author but a consummate platform speaker. While dressing for a talk one day he discovered a sleeve button was missing. Patiently he unbuttoned his shirt and selected another. Again he came to that final button on his sleeve only to discover it too was missing. He angrily swore like a seasoned sailor as he once again unbuttoned his shirt.

He did not notice his wife standing in the doorway. When he finished swearing she repeated word for word what he had said. She hoped to give him a sample of what he sounded like. When she finished Twain remarked, "Dear, you have the words, but you don't have the music."

Want to put some sparkle and fire into your voice?

1. Tape record your side of your phone conversations —listen to yourself.

2. Buy a book on cassette tape and listen to how the reader sounds. Imitate the way the reader sounds.

3. Record a dynamic speaker and listen to the tape. Replay in your mind's ear the words and phrases of the speaker. Then try repeating words and phrases exactly as you heard them.

> **Want to sound enthusiastic?**
> **Be enthusiastic!**

The voice tells it all—Increase the rate, raise the intensity and the pitch. Your voice is at your beck and call whenever you need it. Learn how to use it and remember—enthusiasm is infectious.

Chapter 13   Sit Vs. Stand

> "Any time you get an opportunity to stand, Take It!" — Howard Baker, Jr.

Dare to begin by standing, even when talking to small groups. I say "dare" because the natural tendency is to continue in our "old way"—pulling up a chair and sitting, never to rise except to leave.

Yes, it is best that you sit in with small groups and "belong." I wouldn't advocate standing for the entire time when talking with a small group of people. But... would you have the courage to begin your portion of the meeting by standing and taking charge, then sitting and continuing your communication?

Introductions

Whenever you're in a group setting and the leader requests everybody introduce themselves, stand (button coat if appropriate), pause and then let your eyes lead your voice. First look at a couple of people and then begin speaking. Guaranteed you won't be forgotten—a positive.

Advantages of Standing:

Voice carries better
Stronger voice
Image
Others will be looking up to you
People admire professionalism and courage
Message has more "stick" (lasting memory)

Tip: The ONE Minute COMMUNICATOR

NOTE: The tendency is to hurry. Resist the temptation to rush. Go slow, experience the feeling. You'll gain strength and confidence the more you do it.

The ONE MINUTE Communicator

Chapter 14   **Pronunciation**

Pronunciation is the correct production of sounds, but also includes saying the sounds in the proper order without adding or omitting a sound. It also includes the proper placement of accent.

How do you pronounce the following words:

Envelope	Creek
Coupon	Data
Tomato	Presentation
Economic	Either
Aunt	Ration

Generally we consult the dictionary as to proper usage, spelling and pronunciation. Be aware that the dictionary cannot take into account all of the regional variations or modifications of pronunciations.

Colloquial Usage Dictates

To improve pronunciation:

1. **Become a better listener**—listen to the speech around you. Listen to your role models. Compare your pronunciation with that of successful speakers and business people in your own geographic area.

2. **Get closer to your dictionary**—if your dictionary is more than a few years old, get a new one. Learn to use the primary and secondary pronunciation of words.

3. **Talk about** words with friends—admit you don't know or are unfamiliar with certain words.

Chapter 15 — Variety

In a word, the key to keeping an audience interested in you and your message—**VARIETY!**

Have variety in every aspect of your communication. Lack of vocal variety (monotone) dulls the listener's attention. Failure to have variety of rate, intensity and pitch quickly lulls the listener into an semi-altered state of consciousness. Failure to have variety of visual aids is equally as deadly as the lack of variety of movement and position. Most of all don't forget to have variety in how you use phrases and the length of your pauses.

A good talk is like a suspenseful movie. You must pay close attention and anticipate what might be coming next. When you can predict what's coming, you have plenty of time to take mental "side trips"—easily bored.

Observe the vocal variety and animation people naturally exhibit when they're having fun at a party or engrossed in conversation over dinner in a restaurant. We naturally put variety into our day-to-day communication. For some reason that spontaneity vanishes when we're required to get up to speak. Natural variety is everybody's free gift. The trick is to learn how to become relaxed enough to use it.

**Adult Audiences Aren't Interested in Vanilla.
Add a Little Flavor—
Variety is the Spice of . . .**

Chapter 16 — Lost Audiences

Everybody's experienced the "lost audience" or "lost listener" syndrome. The audience isn't misplaced but rather is no longer paying attention to what you say or do. What can you do?

In conversation we recognize when this is beginning to happen and automatically inject a change of pace or some "spice."

Common "lost audience" symptoms:
- Less eye contact
- Doodling
- No questions
- Lack of attention
- Blank stares
- No (affirmative) nods
- Folded arms
- Empty seats

Most presentations get a free ride for _?_ minutes. That's the audience's checking-it-out period. After that the attention may begin to wane.

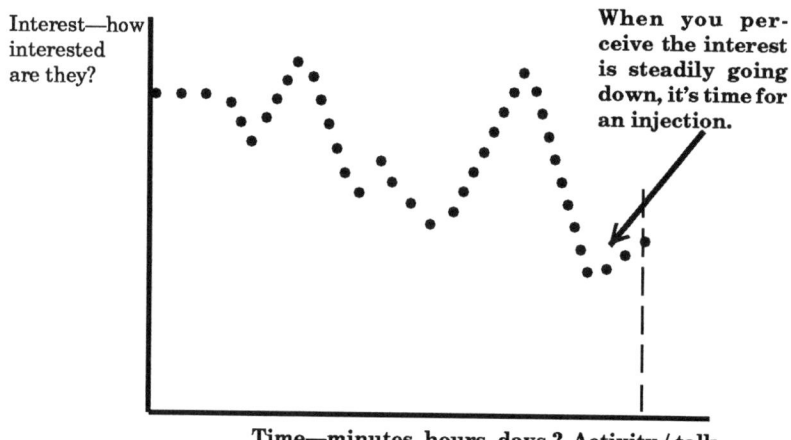

Interest—how interested are they?

When you perceive the interest is steadily going down, it's time for an injection.

Time—minutes, hours, days ? Activity / talk terminated regardless of time.

Change of pace / injections & spices—take a stretch break, team up, brain teasers, puzzles, music, audio visuals, vocal variety, anecdotes, handouts, etc.

Chapter 17 — Lectern, Podium, Dais, Rostrum

Business Doesn't Want A Lectern Talk

Situations which involve a **lectern—reading desk**—are more formal and are the exception rather than the rule in most business settings.

Use a lectern as a place to rest your notes—not as a leaning post or something to grip. Stand evenly on both feet with your weight slightly forward on the balls of the feet. Create baton (hand and arm) angles by placing one hand ahead of the other on the lectern.

Podium—a low raised wall or platform upon which the speaker stands. When there is a lectern on the podium it is frequently called a rostrum—platform or stage for speaking.

The **dais is a high table** in a hall usually in a place of prominence—along the wall or at the end of the room.

The speaking station in a church is called the **pulpit—a high platform or lectern.**

Many become dependent upon a lectern and cannot wean themselves from it. Some cannot even release their "death grip" long enough to gesture. Experiment with movement and learn how to use the lectern as well as how to comfortably get away from it. Try beginning at a lectern and then moving away after concluding your opening remarks—come forward and then lock your posture and remember to stand "stock still." Practice!

Chapter 18 — Meetings

Planning the Program

Good programs and talks don't just happen by accident—they are planned. The talk is planned in its entirety. The most critical element is time. Not the time of the person doing the talking and conducting the meeting but everybody else's time. Give adults a "time" reward.

> **Good Meetings and Talks Don't End on Time!**

They End EARLY!

The most common comment about why meetings and talks go badly is that they are too long. Good meetings are structured just like a well planned program or talk. They have an attention step, a body and a conclusion.

Attention steps can be any form of involvement or something unique or different to set the tone of the meeting. Most meetings are just like poor talks with the openings and endings lacking zip and a middle part that just seems to happen.

Try these :
- Change the time of the meeting
- Change the place, seating, and order of business
- Rotate chairman's duties
- Get as many involved as possible—ask others to conduct the meeting
- Have some "brain" teasers, puzzles, change of pace or focus
- Break into groups and work in teams / switch

Experiment with Change!

Chapter 19 — The Pause Paradox

One of the most difficult aspects of speaking is to utilize the power of the pause. This is especially true in public speaking. We feel a compulsion to speak or make sounds—verbal pauses.

Three wonderful and powerful things happen when you pause:

---

1. **You have time to think.**
2. **Listener(s) reflects back to what was just said.**
3. **Listener(s) anticipates what's coming next.**

Speech rate is comprised of words as well as the time between the words. Experiment with silence. The more you experiment, the more comfortable you become with not speaking. Experiments that have compared trained speakers and poor speakers found that the pauses of trained speakers are longer and considerably more variable in length. This suggests that the main difference comes in the use of more long pauses. Effective communicators control pause length deliberately.

Technique

The ONE Minute Communicator

Speaker's Paradox

> **The most powerful tool the speaker has is to *not* speak.**

Chapter 20 — Tell, Tell, Tell

The easiest way to describe what giving a talk is all about is tell, tell, tell which translates to:

Tell 'em what you're going to tell 'em, tell 'em, and tell 'em what you told 'em.

In its simplest form it is a trite way of getting the job done, but can you use tell, tell, tell as a framework on which to "hang" a talk?

The *opening* portion of the talk is supposed to get the listener's attention as you set up what you are going to talk about.

The *middle* portion is the body of the talk with supporting information and the "meat" of the talk.

The *final* **tell 'em what you told 'em** is the conclusion.

Instead of standing up and saying "Today I am going to talk about . . . ," let your attention step give indication as to what your talk is going to be about. The middle portion of the talk is relatively straightforward with a conclusion that is something other than, ". . .and in conclusion, I have talked about . . . "

Tell, Tell, Tell gets the job done but . . .

Would you like to listen to a series of talks all using the same tell, tell, tell, format?

Get Creative —Be Remembered!

What? No creativity? At least the tell, tell, tell method will work and enable you to get the job done.

Chapter 21

Rhetorical Interrogatives & Non-Words

Rhetorical interrogatives and intercalations are results of talking too fast and trying to speak in sentences instead of phrases. Of the three parameters of speech—rate, intensity, and pitch—rate is most abused. The majority of people talk too fast.

If you are plagued with rhetorical interrogatives and intercalations, slow your speech, use pauses and speak in phrases. The first to fall away as a bad habit will be the intercalations—umm, er, and umm, uhhh, ahhh and any other verbal pauses you use.

Rhetorical interrogatives are a form of self-check to determine your listener is still with you. The trouble is few wait or expect a verbal response from their listener. **Rhetorical interrogatives**—*okay*, *ya know*, and *right* are most common. You may have other favorites.

The more you learn about human communication and speech, the more self-confidence you'll have . You'll no longer feel the need to hurry or rush. You'll cease using intercalations and rhetorical interrogatives.

Rhetorical interrogatives and intercalations
(verbal pauses and non-words)

Ya' know?	**Right?**
Okay?	**uhhh**
errr	**ahhh**
and umm	**?**

Chapter 22   Batons & Gesticulations

Our arms and hands are our batons. Without conscious thought, we aid the thoughts of others with our batons, movement and posture. Gestures are spontaneous. When we try to control our gestures they become stilted and out of sync. Vice President Dan Quayle is a good example of someone who's forcing gestures.

Gestures help to quantify and qualify the meaning of the words we speak. Everybody uses gestures when they communicate. Observe two people deeply engrossed in their conversation and you'll see classic examples of how words are enhanced by baton and body movement.

When we stand and speak we frequently grab onto ourselves and hang on. Men "fig-leaf" and women hold the back of their wrist. We like to keep in touch with ourselves. It gives us comfort. It feels good and secure.

Don't know what to do with your batons?
Pull them up and hold one hand with the other just above the navel, above the waist. Experiment with a variety of baton postures. Try letting your batons hang freely at your side as you speak—not the easiest.

Men—avoid crotch holding, fig-leaf and peek-a-boo baton posture with hands covering crotch.

Women—avoid folding arms across chest or putting hands behind back.

Bigger audiences demand bigger gestures!

> **Get Your Baton Gestures Up and Out**

Chapter 23   The Eyes Have It

Eye contact means "eyeball to eyeball" contact, nothing more, nothing less. It is physically impossible to look into another person's eyes. You can look into one eye or another, but not both at the same time. When we are engaged in a one-on-one conversation, we naturally shift from eye to eye.

Eyes are the windows to the soul.

Eye contact is about watching others to determine the depth of understanding and communication taking place. Our eyes reveal when we understand. The speaker watches for signs that the listener is with him. When the listener demonstrates he is lost, the competent speaker sees this and adjusts the delivery, content or both.

Real eye contact is not planned. The speaker attempts to make eye contact with as many people in the audience as possible. When the group is too large, the speaker uses those closest as a gauge.

> **When you eye contact with another human being, they owe you.**

The most common problem is fleeting to non-existent eye contact. Our eyes go with the phrases we speak. Eye contact is not planned; it is spontaneous. Strive for longer eye contact—practice.

The openings and endings of your communication require 100% eye contact. Remember, eye contact lets you know when real communication is taking place.

Chapter 24 — "Counters" Love Redundancies

FACT: "Counters" Are Always Counting!

Counters count redundancies of voice and mannerism, but are too busy counting and are unavailable to listen to what you are saying.

Avoid being counted by varying your speech and mannerisms—**variety of rate, intensity and pitch thwarts "counters."**

Counters especially love to count the number of times you say "um," "ahh" or "ya' know." They also count how many times you use a redundant gesture or mannerism such as pacing back and forth while talking. Silently they sit counting how many times the speaker passed behind the lectern as he paces back and forth during a staff meeting. Most counters are "closet" counters—they seldom report the results of their counting to anyone.

A tape recorder will help you hear any redundant words, phrases, or verbal pauses. A friend or video taping can help you discover your redundant mannerisms.

Note what happens to your train of thought when you focus on others' redundant words or mannerisms. You cannot focus on the message.

Variety of rate, intensity and pitch Thwarts Counters!

Chapter 25   **Appealing to Others**
Persuasion

We begin using our skills of persuasion before we are born. By adulthood we have developed very sophisticated skills at guiding others in order to accomplish our personal agendas.

Three basic forms of appeal—ethos, pathos, and logos.

Ethos
Ethics, a sense of right and wrong, conforming to moral standards—country, motherhood, apple pie, church, civic responsibility.

Pathos
Sympathy, to suffer, or feel, feelings—sorrow, pity or compassion.

Logos
Logic, reason, linear, and makes sense.

Three forms of appeal. Listen to others as they speak and you will frequently be able to pick out which form of appeal they are using to convince you of their thought, concept or idea.

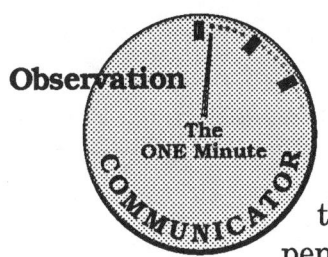

Observe which of the three forms of appeal others may be using to convince you. Be aware that there are not always clear cut lines of difference between the three. We may call on all three depending upon the circumstances.

What's Your Persuasion Preference?

Chapter 26 — Go Toward The Listener
Free-standing

Observe two people engrossed in deep conversation. Both of their bodies lean inward toward one another. The same is true of the sincere communicator who also subtly leans toward the person with whom he is conversing.

It's one thing to stand behind a lectern and talk, but without a lectern you're totally exposed. Business people want you to talk *with* them not at them. Go ahead and begin at the lectern, but plan to move and stay out from behind it. Go *toward* your listeners.

Once you've moved, move to a position and free-stand in front of and slightly to the side of the lectern. Create angles by standing other than "dead center" to your listeners.

Technique
The ONE Minute Communicator

The techniques of *Ready, Set, Go!* apply to freestanding just as they apply to using a lectern. Remember to spend more time standing "stock still" than moving. Keep your knees slightly bent with your weight more on the balls of the feet than on the heels.

Avoid standing in a location which places you perpendicular to your audience. Angles, angles, angles—don't forget the angles!

Chapter 27 — Writing a Talk

The majority of people, when asked to prepare a talk, sit and think, and then begin by putting pencil to paper and writing sentences. We all possess a more natural and easier way to put our thoughts together in order to think and speak clearly and orderly. Many know of this method, but few really work at it. It requires practice to become proficient at brainstorming.

The Quick-Think—Quick-Write Method of Preparing a Talk

1. Brainstorm by writing down as many thoughts as you can about the subject. Make it a storm, not a sprinkle. Strive for quantity and not quality. Quality comes later.

2. Do your audience analysis concurrently or before doing the brainstorm. It's critical to know as much as possible about an audience in order to "fit" your talk to the group. Consider such things as place, time of day, group size, purpose of the talk, etc.

3. Give some thought as to your opening and ending. What's the objective, so what?

4. When possible, put the brainstorm away overnight. Get it out and then select "must cover" items. Additional brainstorming can happen at any time. Select sub-points—they're probably already written down in your brainstorm. You may have to research current facts and figures

5. Write a draft and give it a run-through. Time it. **Practice, practice, practice!**

Chapter 28 Movement

Learn more about movement by observing people moving—how they walk, sit and stand. Executives walk differently than clerks. Notice the difference between competent communicators and those who are less sure of themselves. The competent person walks subtly slower and employs a slightly longer stride.

Standing

A good communicator employs movement which changes the figure-ground relationship for the audience. They move easily and stand still after moving. They know to spend more time standing absolutely still as opposed to constantly being on the move.

Bicycles

Stay off of the "bicycle." Movement feels good because it dumps nervousness. The trouble is, once on the "bicycle" it's difficult to get off. Your words have more power and impact when spoken while standing "stock still."

Sitting

Chair sitting is a two-step process unlike sitting on the toilet (one-step). Observe others sitting and rising from a sitting position and then practice. Be sure to keep your feet and legs still. A great deal of nervous energy is expended through twitching legs and feet.

Batons

Too many gesticulations? Tone it down. Your batons are attached just beneath your chin. You've got the best vantage point to determine if your gestures are wild and out of control.

It takes practice to learn how to control movement!

Chapter 29 — Audience Analysis

Often the most critical element of communication is overlooked. Audience analysis depends upon your topic as well as what you expect the outcome(s) of your talk to be. The more you know about your audience the better you communicate.

What needs to be considered when doing an audience analysis prior to giving a talk? A checklist:

- ❐ **Purpose**
- ❐ **Will there be other speakers?**
- ❐ **Speaking order**
- ❐ **Is there any degree of audience homogeneity?**
- ❐ **Gender**
- ❐ **Religion**
- ❐ **Socio-economic status**
- ❐ **Values**
- ❐ **Needs**
- ❐ **Limitations**
- ❐ **Educational background**
- ❐ **Age**
- ❐ **Occupations**
- ❐ **Political orientation**
- ❐ **Knowledge of the topic**
- ❐ **Interest and attitude toward the topic**
- ❐ **Your reputation**
- ❐ **Your speaking style**

Have you thought about all of the above as they relate to your listeners?

No Surprises!—know as much about your audience as you can.

Chapter 30 — Notes & Manuscripts

Memorization is not advised. The fastest way known to have an "out-of-brain" experience is to memorize. Memorization also detracts from the sparkle and spontaneity of your words.

If you write sentences, you'll read them to us. Most people are not very good oral readers as we seldom practice reading aloud—a skill which takes practice.

Here's the progression—if you've always written sentences, force yourself to write phrases. Next, learn to write only key words, enough to jog your memory. Once comfortable with only key words you're ready to speak without notes, reviewing what you are going to say prior to getting up to talk.

You're not expected to be a computer or machine—use notes, it's normal providing the notes don't come alive and detract from what you are saying.

- **Type or print your notes**
- **Double or triple space**
- **Write only on the top third or half of the page**
- **Use note cards (recommend 5" x 8" size vs. 3" x 5")**
- **Number the pages**
- **All caps or mixed case***
- **Resist playing with notes**
- **Slide pages**
- **Paper shakes? Carry entire tablet or pull your elbows in against body**

* mixed case recommended

Don't fondle, fold, roll, stack or play with your manuscript or notes.

Chapter 31   Humor & Laughter

"What the world needs now . . . is laughter, sweet laughter. Humor and creativity are the gifts we can give ourselves to survive and thrive in the 90's."

Joel Goodman, President, The Humor Project

Everybody wants to be funny. We all enjoy a humorous talk and laughter. We admire those who are able to make others laugh.

Want to be humorous? What do you know about the subject? Where and how to start—Write:

**Humor Project, Inc.
110 Spring Street
Saratoga Springs, NY 12866**

Humor is best when spontaneous. Everybody is funny at one time or another. Most humor is based on human foibles, tragedy, and common experiences.

Most speakers are going too fast (rate) that they miss opportunities to experiment and enjoy moments when they are funny.

If the Audience Laughs—P   a   u   s   e   !

Humor comes from the heart. Attempting to read books of jokes and then tell them usually falls flat. Want to tell a story? Tell it in your own words. If you goof it up the audience may laugh—humor.

Learn from your experiences with laughter and don't hesitate to laugh with the audience if the mood strikes you. We are all our own best source of humor. Learn to laugh at yourself.

Chapter 32 R.I.P.

R.I.P. (not rest in peace) represents the three parameters of speech—**rate, intensity** (loudness) and **pitch**.

Rate

Rate is how fast or slow you speak. People who think quickly also speak quickly. Conversely, those who speak slowly think more slowly. This has nothing to do with the depth of cognition. There is an optimal rate at which you can speak to maximize input to the listener's mind / ear. The optimal spontaneous connected speech rate is an *average* of 159 words per minute (wpm). The key is *average* because a constant rate of speaking renders the listener comatose. The key is to have a variety of rate—not be predictable.

Intensity

Intensity pertains to the softness and loudness of your speech. Like rate, there needs to be a variety of how loud or soft you speak. To speak at the same level of intensity mesmerizes the listener. Certain words want to be stressed or emphasized. Let your feelings be your guide.

Pitch

Pitch pertains to the high or low of your voice. Inflection is a component of pitch. A key to having move vocal inflection (greater pitch variety) is to honor the vowel component of the words. Dare to "give the vowels a vocal ride" by prolonging them. Help your voice become more expressive— "Honor thy vowels to avoid being labeled as monotone."

R. I. P. Variety Creates Interest

Chapter 33 — Memorable Openings & Endings

For some interesting reason we recall the endings and beginnings of events better. The same is true for talks. Getting a rough or poor start is often remembered more than the "meat" of your talk. You can make your opening and ending memorable by employing the use of a prop or visual.

Toward a more creative opening—case history

The business executive was trying to get the office workers to participate in the company golf outing. He chose to speak to the group at the end of the weekly staff meeting. His opening words were something like this, "...I know that you all know there's a golf tournament coming up. How many of you are going to participate?"

A more creative approach—starting:
  Carry a golf club
  Actually hit a golf ball (Wiffle ball®)
  Yell "Fore"
  Display some of the prizes
  Wear golf togs
  Play on the word "birdie"

A more creative approach—ending:
  Hit the golf ball (Wiffle ball®)
  Dump a bucket of balls on the floor
  Give out incentive golf balls
  Pass around a sign-up sheet

Creativity is the Key to Memorable Openings & Endings

Chapter 34 — Monotone

I have never heard a monotone speaker. On the other hand, there are countless people who use very little of their vocal range. These people drone, attach no special meaning to words, and merely speak giving every word the exact same treatment. We call these people monotone.

Words cry out to be spoken differently. Many words have inherent clues in their structure as to how to speak them. Take the word "*smooth*" for example. If you want to convey *smoother* you must stretch the vowel component of the word. To make the word even *smoother* yet, you must stretch the vowel even further. Another good example is the word "*quickly*." To make it convey "very *quick*" you must speak it even *quicker* yet.

Vocal Range

Monotone Tip: Expand your vocal range by practice reading aloud. Read children's stories and let your voice convey the various characters. Experiment, stretch, become enthusiastic. Speak in phrases and utilize more pauses.

Highest voice (includes falsetto)

Notice there is more room to raise your voice (pitch) than to lower it.

Average optimal pitch is generally about one quarter above the lowest level of your voice. This is where your voice works best and is strongest.

Monotone voice stays at or near this level.

Lowest voice

Vocal variety means use your vocal range—honor thy vowels.

Chapter 35 **A Pro *Never* Goes In Cold!**

The statement **A Pro *Never* Goes in Cold!** pertains to overcoming nervousness and making sure your program goes off without a hitch.

If you know you are scheduled to give a talk during a lunchtime meeting, arrive early (before anyone else) and stand where you will be talking. Then move from one corner of the room to another until you have stood in every corner of the room. Now again go stand where you will be giving your talk. It may be on a podium, behind a lectern or free-standing. Stand quietly as you "take in" the room. Get the feel of the room as well as a visual familiarity.

You may need to experiment with:
Lights
Public Address system (PA)
Microphone
Movement on the podium
Lectern (Too high, too low?)
Room set-up (may require changes)
Table or equipment set-up
Speaking order—early advantages
Easel paper (ample?)
Overhead projector—AV equipment
Markers work? (dry, out of fluid)
Movement
Supplies / materials

Be a Pro—Check It Out

Chapter 36
Convince Me!
Formula for Persuasion

Beware! Most of us have had a lifetime of honing our persuasive skills. Even though this formula looks simple and straightforward, be aware that some people may mix the order of sequence.

Five Persuasive Power Points

1. **Attention**—Call attention to a pet peeve or issue of concern. What's "bugging" you?

2. **Need**—Describe the situation as it currently exists. Cite examples, describe the situation—more than one perspective.

3. **Satisfy**—Propose a real and/or workable solution which will satisfy the need for change.

4. **Visualize**—Help others imagine, visualize what conditions would be like if your satisfaction, (solution, method, direction, idea) was in place.

5. **Act**—You must get people to act upon your proposed idea, method, direction or solution. You must get them to commit then and there while "hot" and enthused.

Use the above sequence to formulate and plan your personal agenda.

**Beware!
Persuasive Power Points
Can Come in Any Order**

Chapter 37 — **Question & Answer**

Better Called Question & Response

You may not always have answers but you can always respond. The question and response (Q & R) portion of the talk is usually at the end. It's better to have a few concluding remarks following the Q & R. This allows you to control the length of the Q & R as well as your concluding remarks. Remember, people best remember the first and last parts of your message.

Try these tips:
- Let the audience know if there is to be a question and response opportunity as part of your talk.

- Stick to the time you've allotted for question and response.

- Pause, repeat question or state what you understood.

- Ask for clarification.

Question and Response may involve questions you want to respond to and can, questions you can respond to but would rather not, and those questions you cannot answer.

- Be brief—you may dig yourself a hole with a long response. Respond as directly as possible and give one additional piece of information.

- Don't end on an excuse.

- Be positive about negative questions.

- Step forward, maintain eye contact.

- Control the clock—end on time or early!

Chapter 38   Oral Hygiene

It's a rare friend indeed who will inform you that your breath is offensive, but wouldn't we all like to know?

Self-check your own breath
Wait until an hour after you've brushed your teeth, then run a clean toothbrush over your tongue (extreme back, upper surface) and cheeks, then smell it.

People will seldom tell you how sour your breath is. They find it socially easier to just steer clear of you. They definitely are not available to listen effectively, especially in a close one-on-one conversation.

Mouth odor, sour mouth, halitosis and bad breath are words and phrases used to describe someone whose oral odor is worse that your own.

A major contributor to bad breath is the mucous secreting glands in the throat. Brush your tongue when you brush your teeth. Brush the back portion of your tongue sufficient enough to produce a mild gag reflex. This causes the mucous glands to empty their fermenting contents and aids in producing a "clean" breath.

Good Breath Insurance

Toothbrush—after eating—cheeks and tongue (gag)
Floss—once daily
If you can't brush—rinse and swallow (or spit)

Other countries (Germany, France, Great Britain) sell tongue scrapers, which are as much a part of good oral hygiene as a toothbrush and floss.

Mints & Mouthwash Make Bad Breath Temporarily Taste and Smell Better!—Then Worse!

Chapter 39	N.I.H. Syndrome

N.I.H. is never spoken, it is yelled—loudly! N.I.H. is what you get when you think of a good idea and you take it to your superior. The boss says, rather screams, N.I.H. in your face. N.I.H. translated means, "that will never work, we tried that where I used to work, it's not in the budget, we don't have the money or manpower, what a dumb idea, you've got to be kidding, no way, that will cost us," and a number of other similar responses. Not my idea, forget it!

Abraham Maslow must be mentioned here as he related the individual's self-actualization needs. People like to feel that they are important, that what they have to offer is of some value. People like to participate and be included in the decision-making process.

> **N. I. H.—Not Invented Here**

When you tell people things they fight. When they think they thought of it themselves, it's a good idea.

Choices & Options

When you tell me I fight.
If you ask me, I'll answer.

When I answer, I'm more in control.
When I answer, I reveal myself.

Try making a suggestion or throwing out an idea vs. arrogantly ramming your opinion down another person's throat—it's magic.

Chapter 40

No COIKs
No COIKing Either

COIK is an acronym which stands for the number one breakdown in human communication.

COIK is what you get when you ask for directions from a stranger. COIKed is what you get from your doctor, lawyer, tax accountant, teenager, parents, and just about anybody you talk with.

The one thing you must do is to promise yourself that from this moment on, for the rest of your life, you will no longer allow anybody to COIK you.

The "No More COIKs Oath"

> Regardless of status or station in life,
> No more COIKs
> No more COIKing
> Whether sitting or standing
> COIK no more, forevermore.

Conversely, if you vow to no longer allow others to COIK you then you must vow to avoid COIKing others.

It's okay not to know. Adults are reluctant to admit they don't know. They think that others will think they are "stupid." A better choice of words would be ignorant—not knowing. If you don't know, odds are others don't know either.

Oh, you still don't know what COIK stands for? You have been COIKed as you read this page.

C.O.I.K. = Clear Only If Known

Chapter 41 — Listening Tips
"Quick Fix"

This is a list of tips for improved listening. It's important to realize listening is a lifelong habit. Most of this **"Quick Fix"** is common sense and is intended to remind us how to listen better.

Nobody can make you a better listener. Improved listening habits are a personal endeavor.

- Concentrate
- Relate ideas to the whole
- Anticipate what the speaker will say
- Be prepared to listen
- Anticipate the topic when possible
- Behave like a good listener
- Avoid interrupting
- Be alert and interested
- Seek areas of agreement
- Resist responding emotionally
- Question when you do not understand
- Withhold evaluation—until finished
- Apply "Golden Rule"—do unto others…
- Be patient
- Feedback what you hear

Listening and hearing are *not* the same.

Hearing is the perception of sound. Listening is the association to known/stored information, thoughts, concepts, or ideas. Our hearing acuity declines with age, but our ability to listen is an ongoing learned skill.

We Must Learn to Listen

Chapter 42

"Deadly Dozen" Listening Problems

Observation

Listening— not commonly taught as a school subject. Because we hear we assume we listen. We must *learn* to listen. Listening is subjective and requires individual effort. The **"deadly dozen"** impede effective listening.

Fact Listening

Personal Prejudices

Becoming Emotionally Involved

Uninteresting Topic

Critical of Delivery

Cognition / Speech Rate Differential

Outlining While Listening

Distractions

Faking Attentiveness

Word Familiarity

Easy Listening

Hearing Loss

"With so many intervening variables involved in the listening process—it's a wonder we can understand one another."

Chapter 43 — Playing the Percentages

> *Words Don't Mean*
> *People Use Words to Mean*

Just as there are three parameters of speech—rate, intensity and pitch—there are also parameters of the content or message of speech. The content or message parameters are the words themselves, the tone of voice in which they are spoken, and the accompanying body physiology.

7% of the message is the words
(word meaning only)

38% of the message is tonality
(tone of voice)

55% of the message is the physiology
(visual information / body language)

We best understand face-to-face communication through the total message. The speaker who can utilize all three communicates more fully and with greater ease. Many people are unable to utilize the tonality and physiology aspects of communication. They merely mouth the words. Realize also that some people only perceive the word portion of the message. They are oblivious to the nuances of sarcasm and body language and take people at their word and seldom question—what do you mean?

"But you said..."
"Yes, I know what I said, but that's not what I meant."
"But you said..."
" Oh, forget it!"

Chapter 44 — Asking vs. Telling

"When you tell people things they fight. When they think they thought of it themselves, it's a good idea!"

Howard Baker, Jr. 1980

Pose rhetorical questions to help direct the thoughts of the listener in the direction you want them to go or use **power phrases** such as:

- Stop and think
- Try and imagine
- What would it be like if
- Who among us hasn't
- Did you ever think
- Guess if you can
- Picture in your mind

Rhetorical questions frequently involve Kipling's words: **What, Why, When, How, Where, and Who.**

Minimize "audience fight" by sprinkling rhetorical questions throughout your talk. Rhetorical questions work best when strung together in succession of two's and three's. Remember to cluster them together without pausing. If you pause after asking a rhetorical question somebody in the audience may answer with an answer you don't want.

Begin with rhetorical question(s)

End with rhetorical question(s)

Sprinkle them throughout your talk

A rhetorical question is a question the speaker asks, but doesn't want a verbal answer.

Chapter 45 — Match My Predicates

The effective communicator speaks using words and phrases which help listeners relate to what is being said.

We all have our own perception of the world. Some people respond to words which relate to the sense of vision, while others relate to words and phrases that tap into our auditory or kinesthetic senses.

Effective communication employs phrases which encompass all of the sensory modes. The following lists of predicates represent our most used senses:

Visual	Auditory	Kinesthetic
picture	tune	touch
clear	sound	handle
see	listen	feel
visualize	hear	finger
focus	say	move
illustrate	ask	sharpen
clarify	voice	tap into
outlook	shout	tickle

When people are engrossed in strong communication they naturally use similar words, phrases, language, and communication symbols. Effective communication is a "mirroring" process. Some do it naturally, others have learned to do it.

Match predicates—what happens?

Chapter 46 — Visual Aids

Visual aids are just what they say—visual information which aids the spoken word.

The most common problem with visual aids is visibility. A visual must be clearly seen by all present. That means the person in the furthest corner of the room is entitled to see as clearly as those in the front row.

One school of thought is that printed words and numbers are not considered visual aids. Some feel that a visual aid must be a picture. Actually both are correct under different circumstances. True—a picture helps the viewer to remember better.

Tips!
Incorporate the best of both worlds—utilize words and pictures in your visuals.

Make words into headlines when possible.

Use color for emphasis. (avoid variegating)*
   * Variegated—a different color for each letter

Experiment with layout, borders, boxes, bullets, arrows, shadows, and underlining.

Use Pictures—line drawings, stick figures, pictographs. (pictures which represent concepts or ideas, e.g., bag of money to represent cash)

Lettering takes practice. Use faint-lined easel paper to help keep lettering straight.

Avoid overloading visuals.

Keep it simple!

Chapter 47 — Voice Too Nasal?

Many people are not pleased with the way their voice sounds. Lazy lips and jaw are frequently a contributing factor. Lazy lips and an inadequate oral opening contributes to a whiny nasal voice.

Simple self-test for nasality:

Say the following words contrasting the sound of the words with your nose open and then pinched closed. The words should sound the same with the nose open and pinched closed.

	Nose open	Nose closed	Same	Different
Words:	she	she	☐	☐
	happy	happy	☐	☐
	cat	cat	☐	☐
	puppy	puppy	☐	☐
	Sue	Sue	☐	☐
	duck	duck	☐	☐

There should be no difference between the way the words sound with the nose open or closed. If there is a difference, you can strengthen the muscles of the soft palate. **Try:** blowing up balloons, sustained blowing exercises, drinking <u>thick</u> malts or milk shakes puffing up cheeks and holding.

Weak soft-palate muscles and lazy articulation contribute to a whiny nasal voice. Do the "w" sentence exercises found on page 58. Remember to exaggerate and open your mouth wide as you practice.

The ONE MINUTE Communicator

Chapter 48   **Mumble Mouth**

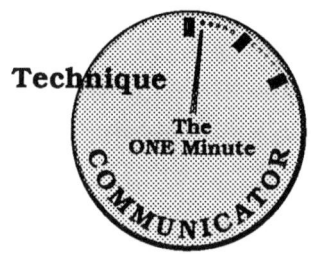

Jeat?
No, jew?
Yup.
Whud jav?
M N X.

We are lazy in our speech and generally take the path of least resistance. For example, use the word *"letter"* in a sentence. Most will say *"ledder"* substituting a 'd' for the 't' in the middle of the word.

Many of the speech sounds are produced in the same manner when it comes to the articulators—lips, teeth, tongue, palate and jaw. For example:

The **f** and **v** are produced in a similar manner. The **t** and **d** share a common method of production as do the **k** and **g**, the **s** and **z**, and **p** and **b**. It's natural for a **d** to be substituted for a **t**. The only difference is voicing.

The key to cleaner enunciation, diction or articulation (synonyms) is to activate (exaggerate) your articulator movement (lips, teeth, tongue, palate, and jaw). Make up a sentence in which all the words begin with the letter "w." Repeat one or two of your "w" sentences while driving to and from work each day (thirty-seconds worth).

"W" Sentence Practice
Whiny Wally walked west with Wendy.
Who walks while whistling?
We wondered which worm would work?

"Seconds a day for a week and someone will comment on the clarity of your speech."

Chapter 49 — Overcoming Your Anxiety

It is of no great comfort to hear that having some anxiety is good and normal. Each person lives with his or her own communication anxiety to varying degrees.

After coaching tens of thousands of people, I have come to the following technique regarding nervousness and anxiety. Learn how to get started like a professional. Your mood, style and overall demeanor affect your audience—be it one or one hundred. It's up to you to take charge of yourself and indirectly take immediate charge of the feelings of others.

Ready, Set, Go! techniques involve where to stand and how to stand. Poise and posture are critical elements which must be mastered.

The majority of speakers say that once they get started they settle down and are less nervous. The key lies in helping the audience realize that they are in good hands. "Relax, I have everything under control so you don't have to worry about me." The confident communicator decreases audience empathy which in turn helps *you* relax.

Drugs and alcohol work. There are even prescription medications—performance drugs (beta blockers such as Propranolol® and Inderal®), but when you don't have them you're back where you started. The only way to overcome anxiety and nervousness is to *get up*—easier if you know what to do. Practice the **Ready, Set, Go!** techniques.

Visualize yourself, your audience, the occasion, the talk, your success, the audience's approval and adulation. **Visualization—powerful stuff!**

The ONE MINUTE Communicator

Chapter 50   **"Mikes"**

Microphones
A Primer

General Rules of Thumb:
- More than 40 in attendance requires a mike
- If your voice projects well avoid using a mike
- Using a mike requires practice / experience
- Stay behind the speaker (feedback—squeal? step back a step or two)
- Talk over the mike not into it
- Keep head of mike below chin—adjust volume
- Mike calls no attention to itself

All microphones are not created equal. Many types of mikes are used in different situations.

Two common types of mikes are:

     cardioid   omni-directional

Types of Microphone Mountings:
    Floor stand   Lavaliere (around neck)
    Boom   Lapel or Necktie
    Table Stand
    Gooseneck (on lectern or table)

A Pro Never Goes In Cold! Arrive early, whenever possible, and check out the P. A. (public address) system. Experiment with volume, tone, squelch, adjustments, and have someone help you listen from different areas of the room.

Chapter 51 — Abused Words

> **There is no such thing as a bad word, only words used in bad taste or at inappropriate times.**

Who helps you grow your vocabulary as an adult? Who corrects our incorrect grammatical constructs and examines the way we speak?

As adults we pick up *"pet"* words just as we did when we were younger. We frequently don't hear the regularity with which we speak our *"pet"* words. It usually requires someone else's ear.

Basically
Of late a popular word which is used with great regularity is the word "basically." Frequently the word "well" precedes basically. In this instance it has become a stall phrase—a stall for time.

Absolutely
Now in vogue and used in lieu of the word yes. You have heard it haven't you? Absolutely!

Clearly
Actually a power word which implies that the statement following is patently clear to one and all. Isn't it clear to you?

Words, especially redundant words, create a case of "mental hiccups" for the listener. Become aware of your favorite words. They will change over time, but don't let them handicap your communication.

(The three example words cited are currently popular "pet" words which frequently create "mental hiccups" for listeners.)

Chapter 52 — Practice Makes Perfect

It matters not how you practice provided you do practice. For some, practice entails doing a complete "dress rehearsal." For others, just standing in front of a mirror is all that is needed.

Suggested Practice Methods:

Mirrors—Okay, but not the best because you tend to stand at right angles facing the mirror. Others seldom see you straight on but rather at angles.

Tape Recorders—Good in that you get to hear yourself speaking and can clean up any phrases which cause you difficulty. Most people will go to the trouble to tape themselves, but then won't make the time to listen to themselves. Taping may also cause the "sparkle" or spontaneity to be absent from your words when you deliver in front of the group.

Video Tape—Better, the video camera catches it all in color with sound and movement. Best done with the camera placed other than perpendicular to where you stand. Remember to create angles even when you're just practicing.

Mental—Best. Use your powers of visualization to see and hear yourself delivering the talk. With practice, you can imagine the audience and their reaction to your talk. This can be done anywhere, anytime.

> **Those who fail to prepare, prepare to fail.**

Practice—*the essential ingredient to becoming a better communicator. Force yourself to do it!*

"Good business women and men are invaluable—those who can communicate effectively are priceless!"

About the Author

Howard Baker, Jr. has written more than twenty books on the subject of human communication and speaking, including listening. He is a subject matter expert on how humans use their most vital tools—their ability to listen and communicate using speech and language.

He is President of **Speakers' Forum**, an international seminar company based in Salem, Oregon. He coaches individuals and businesses, worldwide, in the area of business communication—the foundation for all business interaction and training. His wife, Sherrie, is his business agent who "makes it all happen." Together they write and offer programs which include keynote and general session talks as well as breakout coaching workshops and training. His many books accompany his business communication skill programs.

He is a popular and much sought after platform speaker—recently recognized as one of the top ten speakers at a Society for Human Resource Management (SHRM) Conference. Howard is truly a master of his craft who educates and entertains ("Edutains") audiences worldwide.

Baker enjoys his time at home where he lives with his wife, Sherrie, the children and a doberman they call "Nisha." In his free time he enjoys home projects (he once taught shop) and getting outdoors to enjoy family outings, fishing and gardening.

Howard Baker, Jr.
Business Communication Skills Coach

"If it isn't going to be fun, I don't want to be here! Learning can be fun, a real adventure!"

Fast paced, educational programs that make a major difference in you and your company's business success. Business Communication Skills Coach, Howard Baker, Jr. offers programs to meet your needs.

- Association and Conference—Keynotes/General Session Talks

- Breakouts

- Interactive (practice) workshops

- Coaching sessions—groups and individuals

- Training

- Facilitating

Howard Baker, Jr
Speakers' Forum
P. O. Box 13997
Salem, OR 97309
(503) 399-8460 & FAX

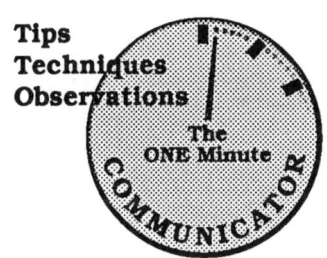